# FUNNY JOKES FOR KIDS: LOUGH OUT LOUD JOKES

## MIKE FERRIS

Knock knock

Who's there?

Pill

Pill who?

It's too early for bed

Q. Why did the snake take a job biting its own tail?

A. It was trying to make ends meet.

What do all hippy cars come with?

Flower steering.

What rental company only lends to women?

Mavis motors.

My schools so broke the principal brought in fat kids, just so someone would buy band candy.

What kind of German car is also a puppet?

An Audi Doody.

Why are open top cars ambitious?

Because they're roofless.

Q. What's a sheep's favorite food?

A. BaaaaaaaBeQue

What do you call a black and white cheerleading outfit? A zebra-ra skirt

How to  put on an opera by Des Valkyrie

What did Dracula say when he bit the truck.

A van to bite your neck.

What do you call a fat muscle car?

A Podge Mustang.

What kind of car never knows the words to a song?

A Humvee.

Q. Why wouldn't anyone believe the big cat?

A. Because he was always lion.

Why do lumberjacks make good helicopter pilots?

They know how to handle a chopper.

Where do cavemen fly on a plane?

Club class.

What channel do pirates take through airport customs?

Booty free.

I'm so scared of flying I don't use runways.

I use runaways.

What's a cowboy's favourite airport?

Idlewild West.

My son is a whizz on the computer, he can find all sorts of confidential information. We're thinking of enrolling him in a Hackademy

What kind of planes carry elephants?
Jumbo jets.

So  the stewardess asks everyone; "can you fly a plane?"
Are we crashing?
No I need a date and I've got high standards.

I've got a pirate car.
Is it fuel efficient?
It gets 100 miles per galleon.

I was going to invest in  a meat by airmail company.
But the steaks were too high.

What do blue bottle stunt pilots fly?

Loop da poop.

Why do sea captains make great pilots?

Because it's plane sailing.

Knock knock

Who's there?

Tatt

Tatt who?

No thinks I'm too young.

How did the bird know it was good at tennis? It was seeded

Where do cars keep their lipstick?

In their clutch.

Why was the teacher so excited about world war two? He was suffering from historya

Q. What comes at the end of a shirt race?

A. A tie.


Knock knock

Who's there?

See

See who?

But you only just got here.


I don't study geometry teachers, what's their angle?


What do you call an Arab teaching maths? Algebra


How did the teacher grow his jacket? In the elbow patch


Why was the boy's bag so heavy? He'd accidentally picked up his rocksack

Teacher: Which element has the Chemical symbol Zn

Franz: Um...errrr

Teacher: Zinc!

Franz: I am Zinking!


Why was coffee banned from the staff room? Because of all the tea-chers


When's the best time to trade insults? At the end of term dissco


Why did the computer stop? Because of the key-bored


In which class do you learn the order of the alphabet? G-ography


What's the laziest item in the playground? The kipping rope


Why did the old computer break? It was on a floppy desk

The Maths teacher wanted to get a huge model of the number Eleven thousand, One hundred and Eleven. But the school couldn't afford it as it was going to cost 5 big ones.

What's the most beautiful part of school? The school-belle

What do selfish people wear to school? A me-niform

How did you know what's in the night sky? By checking the regi-star

Q. Where does the President go when he's stinky?

A. WASHington.

What did Sherlock Holmes investigate as a schoolboy? His pencil case

Why wasn't the builder successful? He didn't do his homework

Knock knock

Who's there?

Day

Day who?

Daylight come and me wanna go home!

Why did the schoolboy's mouth taste of wood? He had chips for lunch

Sally:    Why is everyone so old in this class?

Teacher:  Because it's greyed school

What do posh schools have instead of gyms? James.

What can you play on a really hot day? Hop-scorch

Why was the schoolboy too hot in his uniform? He was wearing a blazer

Why did the handlebars fall off? They saw the sign for 'bike sheds'

Bobby:     Someone just threw an Abacus at me.

Jenny :     It must have been a counter attack.


Why are fish so clever? They're always in schools


When can you learn about car maintenance? Brake time


The Teacher said we could choose where we wanted to swim, It was a Multi Pool choice question


My friend Tommy is really good at Dodgeball  we all miss him very much.


1 in 10 children doesn't understand numbers, but they don't really count


Teacher: Can you tell me what is on the Periodic table?

Sam:     Is it a Periodic Tablecloth?

My Teacher wasn't worried when 50 percent of the children didn't turn up, but that's because he is a 'Class half-full type of person'

Where do boxers get an education? A school of fought

Why can't you teach Cowboys Art?
Because if you ask them to draw they'll fire a gun

What kind of dog always sleeps in doorways? A Labrador.

Bradley:   Are you really winning two games in chess club?
Sally:     I'm not sure I'll just double check

We just bought a German Shepherd dog. It should come in handy if we need to round up any Germans.

Knock knock

Who's there?

Lass

Lass who?

The cattle dummy

My old teacher became a bank robber. He wasn't very successful though. Every time people put their hands up, he thought that they wanted to answer a question.

Teacher: Can you draw me a Nucleus?

Greg: To be honest sir, I don't even know what an Old cleus looked like

Who was James Bond's best friend at school? Ms Dinner Money Penny

Why can't you protest at school? Because they've got marching band.

I want to study a dead language

Latin?

Zombie eeuuurrrgggh

Why is it ok to dissect a frog in biology but not in French?

Teacher: Could you explain Boyles law to me?

Johnny: If you squeeze them they get sore?


What happened when you got an F in art class son?

The teacher opened the window.


How do you greet a dinner lady? Jello!


Our school meat loafs so bad, it's meat coma.

I think the canteens serving rabbit meat in their hoppy joes.


We're studying Henry the eighth, I'm glad we don't have to do the other 7 eighths.


Why aren't school mornings completes? Because some assemblies required.


Our school is so dumb that we get our chicken from KFC minus

Q.        How does a snake get into Hogwarts

A.        Slitherin


Robbie:   Can I make a reservation for the library?

Librarian: No! We're fully booked!


My friend was upset because  he had no paper to draw with. So I gave him a shoulder to Crayon


I needed to learn the accordion. The teacher was really busy, but he squeezed me in.


Why are all cars fat?

Because they've got a trunk with a spare tyre.


The principal can always keep his eye on you he's got hundreds of pupils


I don't trust my maths teacher he's far too calculating.

The coach must be enormous, if he can carry the whole football team to the game!

What do you have to look at longest to understand? The peeriodic table

I wanted to go to Video Game College but I didn't have enough credits.

My friends and I sing together, and stick together. We're in the Glue club.

Teacher: Do you think John needs homeschooling?

John's Mum: No I think John's house is clever enough already

We're studying the history of snakes, it's hissstory

I can't remember if I'm doing omelettes in cookery, or Hamlet in English.

What school did Sherlock Holmes goto? Elementary Watson.

I only studied maths because I heard there was going to be pie.

Our geography teacher is so old, her globes flat.

Q. Where do vampires buy their art supplies?

A. Pencil-vania.

How tall do you have to be to go to high school?

Even Sherlock Holmes couldn't solve the mystery meat.

Knock knock

Who's there?

Sool

Sool who?

Shouldn't you be on the Enterprise?

Q. Where to bed bugs trade stocks?

A. On the flea market.

These beans are so old, they're has beens

What kind of sauce is this?

It's the number one source of diarrhoea

Look how well I'm doing at Latin dad!

Son it says how often you've been late in!

Why should I take physics seriously? I don't get the gravity of it.

My schools so broke our exchange program.

Swopped 6 pupils for a coke machine and a printer.

Q. What did the ref say to the cheating turkey?

A. FOWL!

The one time we pray at school is before lunch, pray we survive it.

Teacher: Can you name a Nursery Rhyme?

Julie: Bursary!

These burgers are agreeable, they've got no beef.

I've just been to a class, where everyone was making pots and they were all dressed as Wizards. It was a Harry Pottery class.

Q. Fly did the building float away?

A. It was a light house.

These hot dogs are so bad I'm calling a vet.

My schools so broke we're studying; English, maths and bee biology together.

2 bee or not 2 bee.

My teachers an idiot he was talking about the founding fathers. It's finding and what were they even looking for?

Q. What's the heaviest type of rain?

A. Reindeer.

If you learn maths you'll rule the world.

How?

Divide and conquer!

I went to a nomad school last year

Was it tough?

It was in tents.

No I won't join the glee club

I can't see what all the song and dance is about.

When was the light bulb invented?

After the dark ages.

Q. Why did the millionaire quit her job as a baker?

A. Because she didn't kneed the dough!


We're studying the stamp act, I think I've got it licked.


Q. What don't Jewish dinosaurs eat?

A. Jurassic pork.


Who's the most native American pupil? Runs with scissors.


Knock knock

Who's there?

Sh

Shwho?

Well hurry up and drop the other one


Our schools so broke we have a baseball zirconium.

Q. Why did the man get fired from the deli?

A. He didn't cut the mustard.

My school's so broke when we sent money to the developing world they sent it back.

Why wouldn't King Arthur go to a bar? He preferred a Knight in.

My school banned mobiles

When the phones got smarter than the kids.

Q. Why didn't the candy bar get into the party?

A. Because he was choco-late.

Knock knock

Who's there?

Twittwa

Twitwawho?

You still got those darn owls!

Q. How to trees get into facebook?

A. They log in.

My school's so broke our astronomy class studies the stars on e tv.

Q. What does a duck put in its soup?

A. Quackers!

Our school sacked the head teacher, I think that shows a lack of principle.

Why are we studying rabbits in math class? We're doing multiplication.

Q. What's a dog's favorite part of a gold course?

A. The ruff!

Knock knock

Who's there?

Yah

Yah Who?

Yeeha!

Q. What's the fastest flu symptom?

A. A running nose.

Q. Who is top of the barnyard pop charts?

A. Lady Baa Baa

Why did you bring a microphone and guitar to maths class?

I thought there was going to be a pop quiz.

Q. How do you know bugs are religious?

A. They're all in sects.

Q. What happened to the sick frog?

A. It croaked.

Knock knock

Who's there?

Cash

Cash who?

Go away I have a nut allergy


Q. Why did the broken padlock cry?

A. Because it was insecure.


Dad can I borrow your credit card?

Why?

We're studying biology.


Q. How do you get fired from a job as a ski instructor?

A. Let your performance go downhill.


My Cat now wants all his food boiled,  Well that's a whole new Kettle of fish.

Q. What's the scariest insect?

A. A Zom-Bee.

Why did the Chicken flap so much  Because he had some hotwings'

I got myself a dog called Patch.  He helped all my other dogs to give up smoking

Q. What's a caveman's favorite type of pizza?

A. Stone baked

My dog is such a liar, he's a golden deceiver.

Q. Why shouldn't baby cows slice the turkey?

A. They can't calve it.

Which animal loves the feel of skin? The mole

Q. How to prisoners stay in touch?

A. On their cell phones.

What did the hippy tiger do? Became a tie-dye-ger

Q. What did the cat play in the orchestra?

A. Puuurrrrrr-cussion.

What was Julius Caesar's favourite game at school? Conquers

What do feet most love to dance to?

A socksophone

Q. Why did the pepper go to prison?

A. A Salt

What do donkeys use instead of a see-saw?

A hee-haw

Q. What's a baker's favorite movie?

A. Pie School Musical

What did the confused fireman wear?

A blaze-er

Q. What's a spaceman's favorite number?

A. Astro-nought

How to speak French by Harley Francais

Did you hear about the hat that was three styles in one?

It was a hat-trick

Q. What type of insect is best at English class?

A. A spelling bee.

My budgies so depressed he says "who's a pretty boy? Not me.2

Q. Why did the grizzly have no friends?

A. He was unbearable.

My Dogs got no Knows!

Really? How does he spell?.

Have you seen  my Catfish? me neither so I don't know where he's getting those kippers from.

Q. How do cats show they like something?

A. Give it a round of a-paws!

I can't take my dog to see Shakespeare, as soon as he hears about two bees he runs off.

Q. How do patriots get through snow?

A. A Sledge of Allegiance

However high you drop a Cat from it always get's annoyed

What animal meditates? A chipmonk

How did the silly boy try to connect his TV and DVD player?

A scarf-lead

What did the left hand say to the right hand when they played in the snow?

'This is so glovely'

How do you get the attention of the end of a skirt?

Say 'a-hem'

Q. Why was the buffalo procrastinating?

A. To bison time.

What did the shoe say when the other shoe was talking too much?

Put a sock in it

What is kept in Willie Wonka's wardrobe?

Joompah-loompahs

How did the coat feel like it was giving the wearer a hug?

It was a coat of arms


No-one could win the terrible game of tug-rope…

It was a tie


Is that a sheep dog? No he cost $500!


Why are budgies like political parties ? They've got a left wing, a right wing and a bird brain in the middle.


Q. Why didn't the fuzzy Australian animal get into college?

A. He didn't have the KUALAfications.


My snake wrote his autobiography, it was a hiss and tell story.


My snakes so fat it's a pie-thon.


Cats always have an alibi, they never go anywhere  without their tail.

I've got myself a Lizard.... Lizard.... Lizard.  Hang on, I think there's a 'Gecko' in here.

Q. Where do animals go to study the brain?

A. The Hippo Campus.

How do you get a cat out of a tree? Tell him its covered in bark.

Why are german cats shortlived? They've got nine lives.

My cats so fat he can only get his head through the cat flap.  I call him Justin.

Q. What part of the kitchen is best at math?

A. The counter.

Why did the pig learn karate? So he could give a pork chop

Which is the easiest Dog to take to the vets?

Boxers because they are used to Jabs

What do you call a drawing of a poodle eating spaghetti?

A Poodle Noodle Doodle

Why do wolves get upset if they lose at cards? They hunt in packs

What animal can you rent? A pig-let

Which bird is best at saving money? A budgetrigar

Why are bees so successful in the army? They always earn their stripes

Q. Why do cats take so long to sign a contract?

A. They like to read every claws.

How does a cat cook? It uses its whiskers

How do you recognise an elephant's writing? It's in an elefont

What do cats sing along to? Mewsic

What animal loves playing the saxophone? A bluesbird

Which animal makes the best secret agent? A spyder

Q. Who are the warmest competitors at the Olympics?

A. The long jumpers.

Why do cows never get parking tickets? They always moove

Which dog can understand morse code?  A dot dot dash-hund

Which animal loves dancing? The discow

My cat does so much scratching that I've got him a job as a DJ

I told my Postman 'No flyers!'. And the next day he bought me two Ostriches and an Emu.

I can't train my pet Cockerel today, But I will add it to my 'To Doodle Do' list

My Pet Chicken has just written his Autobiography. Next week he's having a 'Book Book Book' signing.

Which animal eats from fish and chip shops? The batterfly

Where do explorers learn how to eat well?
In Captain Cook-ery class

What computer do frogs use? The Lilly-pad

Knock Knock. Who's there?
Woo.
Woo Who!
At last someone is pleased to see me

My Pet Horse has two bad legs, so he's always using the good clop bad clop routine.

What's the name for a sociable pigeon? A pige-out

Q. What TV show are seamstresses scared of?

A. The Walking Thread.

What do Turtles like to do on their days off  - Go Terrapin bowling

I said to the Apiarist.  Do I have to pay for that one that just escaped? He said no, that one's a 'Free Bee'

What's the happiest kind of cat? A purrrsssian

My cat signed a contract not to cough up any more hair, Well it was more of a furball agreement.

Where do baby cats sleep on holiday? In a kittent

Why are bees so famous? There's always a buzz about them

Which animal is best at D.I.Y? A turtool

What do you call a male sheep? A heap

Knock Knock

Who's there?

Paul

Paul who?

Pull the door open, it's cold out here!

What bird is best on the water? The c-row

Johnny: Why won't you tell me where your bees are hidden?

Billy: Swarm to secrecy

My cats called ow, how do I know? When ever I tread on his tail he says "me ow."

When I was at school if you cheeked a teacher I got hit with a wooden board.

Lucky you I just get bored.

Why can't cats dance? They've got 2 left feet.

Where do dogs meet their friends on line? Butt book.

It's easier to get a cat out of a tree then a cat out of a tree

Knock Knock

Who's there?

Terry

Terry who?

Terrible weather out here, hurry up!

What do cats order in starbucks? A cattuccino

My cats so glam he's got a glitter tray.

I threw a stick 2 kilometres, and my dog brought it back.

Talk about 'far fetched'

Just because your parrot can talk, doesn't mean its got anything to say.

Q. What is God's fairy dairy product?

A. Baby Cheeses

I tried to follow my pet Cat wherever he went. But I ended up getting in a flap about it.

What do Shakespeare say when he was thinking about buying a cat? "tabby or not tabby?"

My cat loves rap music so much, I've bought him his own scratching post.

What's the dullest part of a computer?

The keybored

Where do cats do their tweeting? In their twitter tray.

My Pet Frog needs to go on a Diet so I've put him on the 'No Fly' list.

What's the shyest fish? A koi carp.

Knock Knock

Who's there?

Dan

Dan who?

Down here, I'm very short!

What's a wasp's favourite sport?

Rugbee

How to fry anything by Chris Pee


How do footballers send letters?

Through the goalpost


How to massage People by Hans On


Why was the monkey drunk?

He'd been at the monkey bars


Why couldn't the girl stop playing hockey?

Hockey sticks


How did the naughty puddle introduce itself?

'My name's mud'


Q. Who do you call when you run out of sandwich meat?

A. The Ham-ergency Services.

What kind of pasta do zombies eat at school? 100% whole brains.

What game can you play when you've got a cold?

Statchoos

How does a DVD get exercise?

By skipping

Knock Knock

Who's there?

Mickey

Mickey who?

Me key's broken, let me in

How does the bird get up high?

It s-wings

What does a king like best in his pencil case?

The ruler

Why can you hear a doorbell?

Because of bellectricity

If we get a jelly fish dad can we also get an icecream fish?

Introduction to astronomy by Stella View

My Mum told me to do some home-work…

So I washed the windows

Why are some words in books longer than others?

Because they tell the author 'letters in!'

How to run for ages by Mary Thon

When I went to school we learned the differences between triangles

Only because you had to build the pyramids in gym class

What was the tree told when it wore antique jewellery?

'You can tell a tree's age by its rings'


Where do you keep old maths books?

In mathem-attics


Why can't desks face the other way?

Because sksed isn't a word


Q. Why did the frog have to go to work?

A. Because his car was toad.


Why is science sometimes difficult?

Because of the chemystery


How to be a tyrant by Dick Tater

When I was your age we were so broke all I had for lunch was a sandwich of two slices of bread and hope for filling.

My brothers so stupid, he brought a lawn mower to school so he could cut class.

How to panic by Fran Tic

When I was a boy we were so poor our baseball field had a zirconium instead of a diamond.

Son when I was your age; we had to walk 10 miles to school and 10 miles back again.  Didn't matter if it was raining or snowing. And it taught me one important lesson.

What lesson was that dad?

Where the school bus stop was.

How to rob banks by Hans Up

What happens after we all fall down in ring o'roses?

Ring a'rises


Q. Why is the coffee always lonely?

A. Because all the tea leaves.


When I was your age I got fit and earned money delivering papers

You must have dad they were on stone tablets back then


When I was your age we had to make our own entertainment

Yeh but you had diplodocuses to slide off of dad


Dad you're so old when you went to school there were only 6 stars on the

flag.


Son I was at school things weren't so easy.  At recess we had to chase the monkeys off the monkey bars.


Back when I was at school we had respect for our teachers

I can respect them for putting up with you.

Q. How do ducks advertise?

A. On a bill board.


How to feel bad by Gill T Feeling


When I went to school we learned all about the founding fathers

You went to school with the founding fathers dad

27006492R00029

Made in the USA
Middletown, DE
09 December 2015